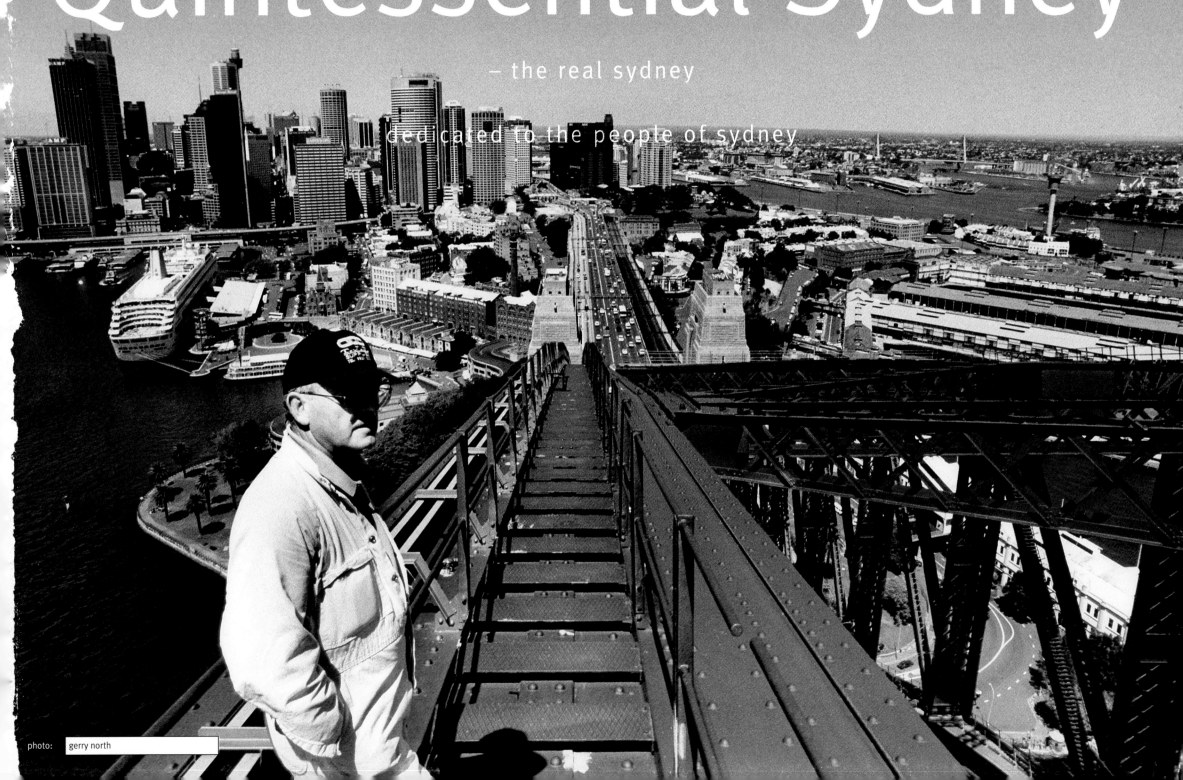

Quintessential Sydney

— the real sydney

dedicated to the people of sydney

photo: gerry north

summer thunderstorm
anzac bridge

photo: steven siewert

first published in 1999 by city media services pty ltd

57 cowper wharf road wolloomooloo nsw 2011 sydney australia

tel: **61 2 9368 1462** fax: 61 2 9357 4394

email: cmsdm@ozemail.com.au

acn 003 795 284

author gerry north

quintessential sydney – the real sydney ISBN 0-646-37429-X

photographers

CHRIS IRELAND

SCOTT WAJON

MALCOLM BELL

MAZZ IMAGES

EROS CANDUSSO

GERRY NORTH

MARCO BOK

GARRIE MAGUIRE

STEVEN SIEWERT – sydney morning herald

STEVE CHRISTO – sydney morning herald

NICK MOIR – sydney morning herald

ANDREW TAYLOR – sydney morning herald

WILLIAM YANG

DAVID MOORE

PETER NIELD

CRAIG HASSALL

sponsors

without their assistance this book would not have happened

CANBERRA PRESS

EDWARD DUNLOP PAPER CO

4 COLOUR GRAPHICS – FILM MAKERS

Quintessential Sydney

the real sydney

Quintessential Sydney is a photographic exposé of how the people of Sydney relate to their environment, thereby creating its personality.

Sydney has such magnificent beauty, especially around the harbour and beaches, that it is easy to be taken in by the obvious tourist sights. *You won't find a Sydney-sider who does not love the Sydney Harbour Bridge – in fact the sight of it when flying home can easily bring a tear to the eye.* But if you are like me, you want to feel and understand the culture of places visited by stripping away tourist cliches to discover how the populace really live. Hopefully after reading these images you too will understand how it feels to be a local.

A Sydney local could be any nationality. Every nationality in the world is represented here, and as a result Sydney has rich and diverse gourmet, arts and social expressions. I'm sure some of the images contained in *Quintessential Sydney* will even surprise some of the locals when they see just how diverse our society really is.

The Australian idiom "Give them a fair go," still thrives in Sydney, resulting in one of the most tolerant cities in the world. This freedom *to-be-what-you-want-to-be* has created a tribal attitude in the populace. This tribal existence has also developed due to the topography of Sydney with pockets of people, separated from other pockets of people, around the harbour and hinterland.

Sydney life is about getting outside as the weather is glorious – *Autumn and Spring are my favourite seasons with temperatures in the 20's with the city bathed in glorious golden sunlight.* Being involved with what is happening, attending an outdoor concert, basking at the beach or breakfast on weekends with friends is what Sydney life is. There is also an eccentricity among the people as you will see in these images.

Sydney will embrace the Olympic Games and what an exciting city this will be in the year 2 000. But after the races have been run and the dust has settled we will go back to the life we adore. This might be watching the awe inspiring New Year's eve fireworks on Sydney Harbour, yelling, "SYD-------NEY" at a game of Aussie Rules, running in the City to Surf or standing at the Heads to watch the start of the Sydney to Hobart yacht race.

The photographers for this book were selected for their ability to capture soul and content. Although in no way claiming to be definitive, *Quintessential Sydney* was viewed by the photographers with the same mind set – **let me show you with my eye the city we live in.**

This book will take you on a journey of people and places that will reveal the soul of of this great city and document our way of life for future generations.

Gerry North

beaches/harbour

*"I'm originally from Melbourne. I came to Sydney got married and now have a beautiful baby boy.
Living in Sydney means my boy will grow up with sunshine, sand and waves. I truly love the beaches here."*

Cathy Gallagher. Age 34. Marketing Manager.

Quintessential Sydney

first swim of summer
bondi

photo: william yang

bondi

bondi

Photo: marco bok

narrabeen

photo: gerry north

bondi

Photo: marco bok

16

photo: marco bok

womens' pool
coogee

Photo: mazz images

18

photo: marco bok

photo: malcolm bell

tamarama bay

photo: gerry north

the gap – lovers leap
watsons bay

photo: gerry north

Photo: marco bok

redleaf pool

Photo: gerry north

tribes

Quintessential Sydney

"When I first came down from Brisbane it struck me immediately you can be whoever you want to be here. I just love Sydney for that."

Sue Beyer. Age 27. Graphic Designer

Quintessential Sydney

spanish quarter
liverpool street

Photo: marco bok

40

Photo: marco bok

48

HOMES
Sumerlin
LOT
SOLD
VALUE
FOR
YOUNG HOMEBUYERS
(02) 822 1155
Lic. No. 402241

Glenmore Park

photo: scott wajon

Photo: scott wajon

Charlie Magist

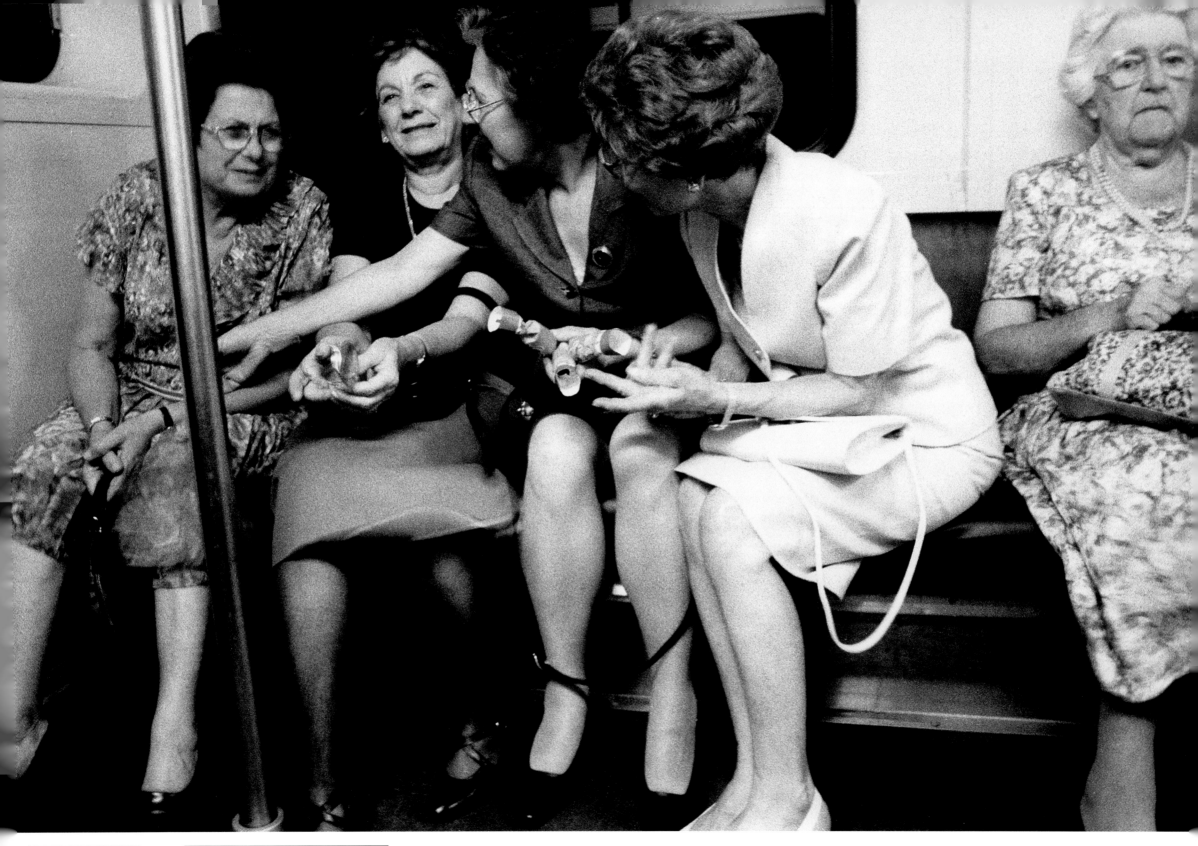

landsdowne hotel
broadway

Photo: scott wajon

58

habib dib and samira
carlton

photo: steven siewert

photo: william yang

photo: marco bok

Photo: marco bok

events

"Sydney people love to do lunch and if things get too much you can always just go to the beach. It's a truly great place to live."

Stuart Coffey. Age 27. Computer Analyst.

Quintessential Sydney

start of the rat race
cbd

Photo: steven siewert

nude surfing
competition – bondi

photo: gerry north

annual dog race
surry hills

photo: scott wajon

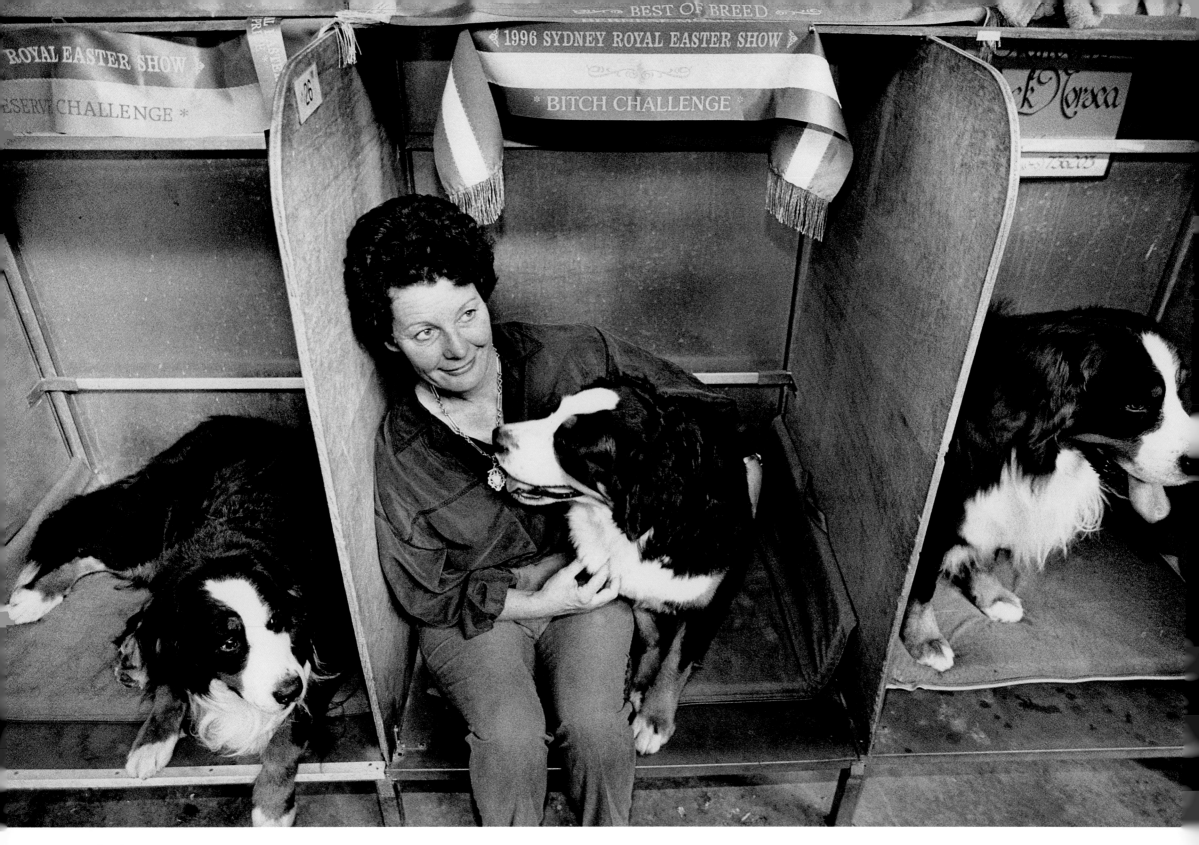

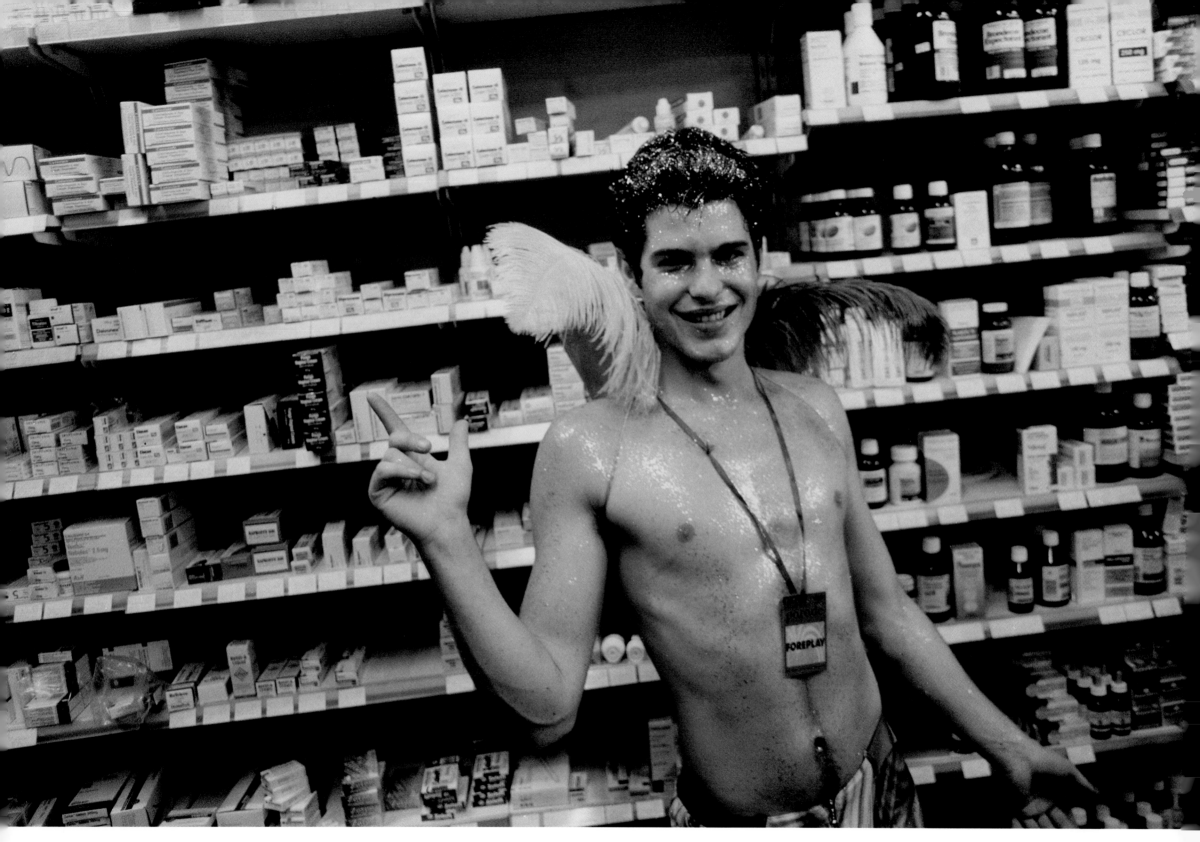

bed races
kings cross

Photo: gerry north

greek epiphany
ceremony – botany bay

photo: nick moir

Esso Opera in the Park

places

"Sydney is beauty amid chaos, excitement amid stress, tolerance amid diversity."

Cliff Bromiley. Age 42. Civil Engineer.

Quintessential Sydney

anzac bridge

photo: david moore

north sydney pool

Photo: scott wajon

archibald fountain
hyde park

photo: chris ireland

avenue of trees
hyde park

photo: gerry north

circular quay station

DONT EVEN THINK

finger wharfs
millers point

photo: garrie maguire

harry's pie shop
woolloomooloo

photo: gerry north

photo: gerry north

This crate always remains the property of the

S.W. FISH MARKETING AUTHORITY

as owner or agent.

Unauthorised users are liable for prosecution.

PENALTY $200

sweat and leisure

"Sydney is such a physical town. It is like if you don't sweat then you shoudn't be here."

Allison Tomridge. Age 36. Shop Assistant.

Quintessential Sydney

bondi

Photo: scott wajon

college street

photo: scott wajon

the domain

photo: eros candusso

street life

"This is my fourteenth visit to Sydney. The people here are so kind and helpful and you guys are just so relaxed. I love your expression, 'N o worries'. I'll be back."

Bob Pugh. Age 73. Lives in New York. Retired Travel Consultant

Quintessential Sydney

broadway

photo: gerry north

kings street traffic
protest

photo: gerry north

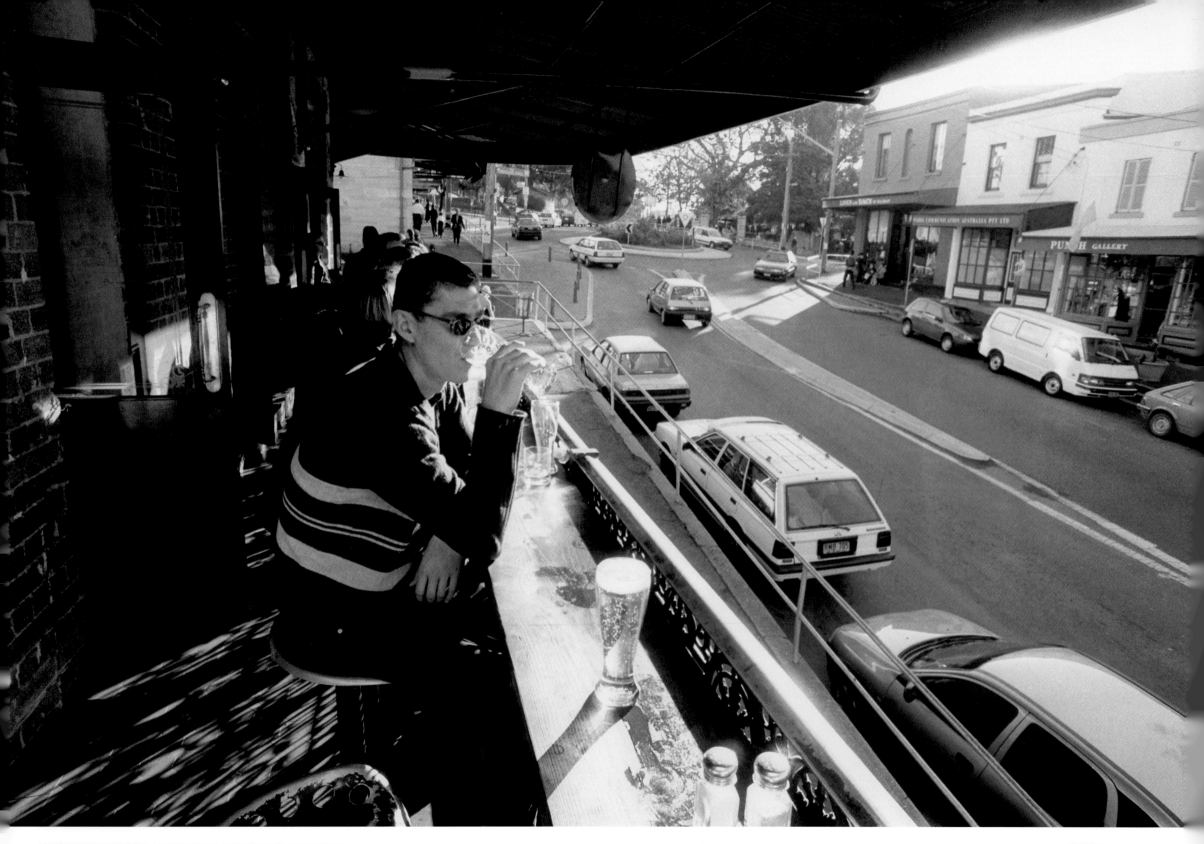

photo: steven siewert

cinema precinct
george street

photo: marco bok

Photo: marco bok

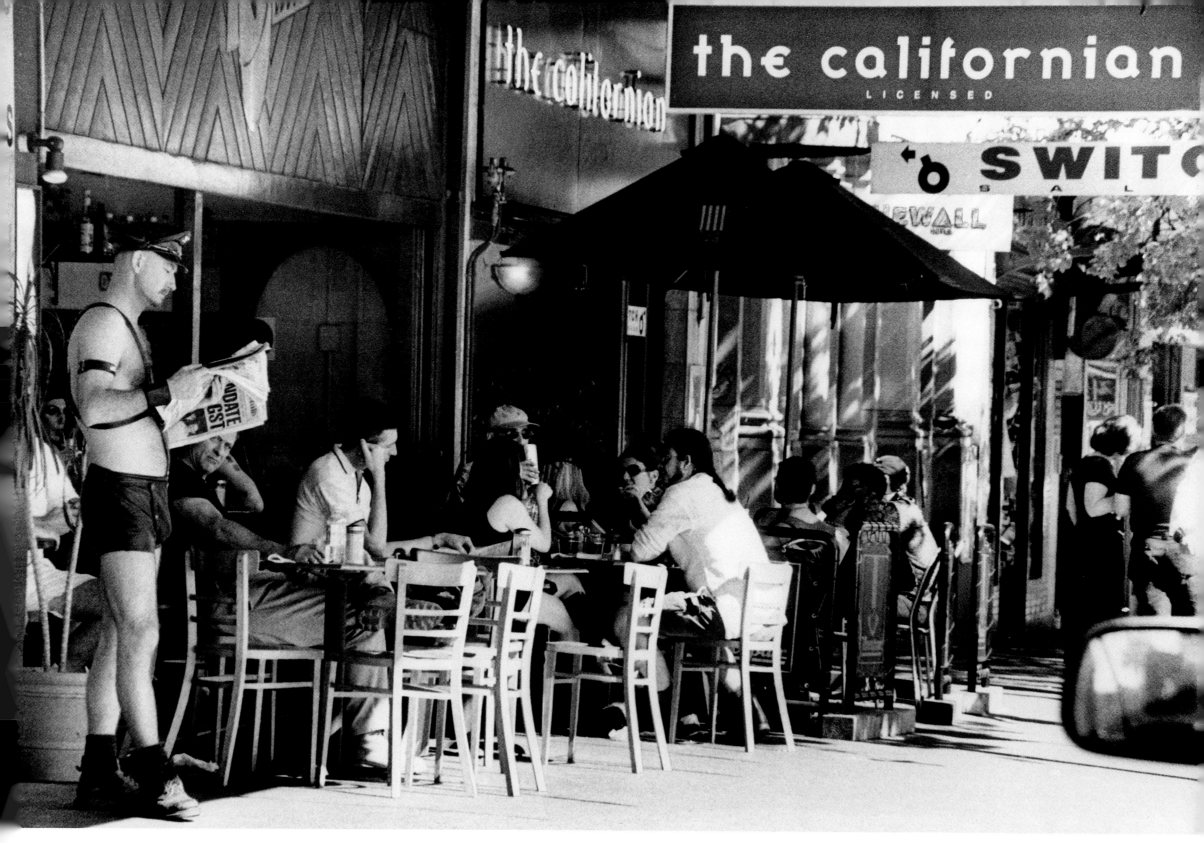

macquarie street   photo: scott wajon

redfern   photo: marco bok

under the flight path
sydenham

Photo: nick moir

night roller bladers   photo: steven siewert

Some men are born with style.

Others simply have it delivered each month.

detail from a photo by: marco bok

book design and layout

GERRY NORTH

black and white film processing

PHOTO TECHNICA & THE PHOTOGRAPHERS THEMSELVES

film separations

FOUR COLOUR GRAPHICS

printed in australia by

CANBERRA PRESS

paper stock supplied by

EDWARD DUNLOP PAPER -TEXT SAPPHIRE DULL 150GSM

published

first published in 1999 by city media services pty ltd

57 cowper wharf road wolloomooloo nsw 2011 sydney australia

tel: 61 2 9368 1462 fax: 61 2 9357 4394

email: cmsdm@ozemail.com.au

acn 003 795 284

author gerry north

quintessential sydney – the real sydney ISBN 0-646-37429-X

special credit photo page 52 reproduced with permission of the mitchell library, state library of new south wales.

sponsors

without their assistance this book would not have happened

CANBERRA PRESS

EDWARDS DUNLOP PAPER

4 COLOUR GRAPHICS – FILM MAKERS